Rational Emotive
Behavior Therapy

Depression

Revised

Tim Sheehan, Ph.D.

The following titles compose the complete REBT learning program. Each is available in booklet, workbook, CD's, and DVD format:

Understanding • *Anger* • *Perfectionism*
Anxiety and Worry • *Depression* • *Shame*
Grief • *Guilt* • *Self-Esteem*

Hazelden
Center City, Minnesota 55012-0176

ISBN 13: 978-1-56838-946-2

The stories in this workbook are composites of many individuals. Any similarity to any one person is purely coincidental.

About the workbook
To people in recovery from chemical dependency, becoming depressed can be an extra hindrance. This workbook provides an effective format to guide recovering people in overcoming depression with Rational Emotive Behavior Therapy (REBT).

Dr. Albert Ellis, who first articulated Rational-Emotive Therapy (RET) in the 1950s, changed the name in the 1990s to Rational Emotive Behavior Therapy (REBT) to more accurately reflect the role behavior plays in gauging changes in thinking. While the therapeutic approach remains the same, the pamphlets, workbooks, audios, and videos in this series have been changed to reflect the updated name.

About the author
Timothy J. Sheehan, Ph.D., is Vice President, Academic Affairs, for the Hazelden Foundation's Education Division.

Dr. Sheehan holds a Doctorate Degree in Clinical Psychology and has held numerous positions over the past twenty years at Hazelden, including leadership roles in clinical psychology and health care services, as well as administrative roles in adult, youth, and transitional care. He is the author of a sequence of pamphlets and workbooks addressing the application of Rational Emotive Behavior Therapy for depression and shame as well as *Facing an Eating Disorder in Recovery* and *Freedom from Compulsion: An Eating Disorder Workbook*. He is also the author of "The Disease Model" in McCrady and Epstein's *Addictions: A Comprehensive Guidebook*. He is a professor in Hazelden's Graduate School in Addiction Studies and an adjunct associate professor in the graduate school of psychology at St. Mary's University of Minnesota.

Introduction

This is a workbook designed for people who struggle with the dual problems of depression and chemical abuse. Drawing on Rational Emotive Behavior Therapy (REBT), we will learn how

- our thinking and behavior cause feelings of depression
- we can feel better by changing our thinking

Before we can recognize and do anything about depression, we need to know what it feels like. Some of us have felt overwhelmed by melancholy feelings, while others have suffered from long periods of sleeplessness and fatigue. Depression affects not only how we feel but also our thoughts and behaviors. Some depressions are more severe than others. Many depressions are short-lived and reactions to losses that we have suffered and stubbornly refused to let go of.

Another type of depression seems to be built into the very nature of our character. We suffer as a result of negative beliefs—we feel a lack of worth, see our future as bleak, and view ourselves as social rejects. While the dynamics of depression may vary, modifying our attitudes and changing our behavior are likely to ease our discomfort and help us to cope.

Chemical dependency and depression

For those of us in recovery from chemical dependency, depression can hamper our efforts at maintaining gains we have already achieved. Depression not only feels disturbing and scary, it can also trigger self-defeating behaviors such as a return to excessive drug use, pathological gambling, compulsive eating, or really, any compulsive behavior.

In the pages that follow, we will

- participate in self-awareness exercises
- learn how to change our thinking
- learn how to change our self-defeating behaviors

Let's get started.

The *ABC* process described in this workbook is based on the work of Dr. Albert Ellis and his Rational Emotive Behavior Therapy.

Developing self-awareness

Many of us grew up believing that *situations* in our life *made* us feel depressed, that we had no choice about how we felt. Consequently, we looked for ways to change how we felt. Sometimes this included doing things that dulled the pain but did nothing to help us solve our problems. Few of us realized that it was actually our thoughts that played an important role in how we felt.

Thoughts ⟶	*Feelings*
My wife should be more loving and attentive.	depression
It's awful to feel alone and isolated in my own home.	depression
This is just more evidence that I'm an unlovable, worthless worm.	depression

What are some of your thoughts about a particular situation that trigger feelings of depression? Write them in the space provided.

Situation:

_____

Thoughts that trigger feelings of depression:

_____

_____

Next, for contrast, list in the following space some thoughts that leave you feeling more content, satisfied, or happy about the situation.

_____

_____

Some of us confuse our thoughts with our feelings. Feelings are combined mind and body sensations that may create an urge to do something that results in a particular behavior or action. "When I feel depressed, I just want to escape and be all by myself." Depression is the feeling; the resulting urge is to escape. Thoughts are the sentences that run through our mind and are actually the core of our feelings of depression.

Thoughts trigger feelings →
           Feelings create urges →
                      Urges motivate behavior

Feelings are usually described in one word such as *mad*, *sad*, *glad*, or *scared*. List in the following space words you use to describe your feelings of depression.

- When I'm depressed I feel

_____

_____

Next, think about how you are feeling now, or recall a time when you were particularly depressed. Describe the urges you felt as you complete the following sentence.

- The last time I felt depressed, I wanted to

_____

_____

You might find that if you acted on these urges, you would actually feel *more* depressed. Excessive drinking or drug use, compulsive overeating or gambling, help destroy our self-esteem. Escaping, isolating, or running away rarely helps us to solve problems of depression. The more we drink, the more depressed we feel. The more we isolate, the more time we have to think of how miserable we feel.

A pattern of negative thinking often triggers and reinforces this self-defeating cycle.

Positive thinking	*Neutral thinking*	*Negative thinking*
I'd hoped for more out of that client. But really, landing that business deal was icing on the cake. What an achievement!	I'm reasonably satisfied with landing that business deal. Often I need to delay what I want now in order to have what I want later.	I never get what I want, and that business deal is no exception. What an awful situation. I can't stand this anymore.

Positive thinking helps us to enjoy life. It is a problem only when it is unrealistic, setting the stage for disillusionment. Negative thinking consistently triggers and reinforces feelings of depression.

Think of a situation you felt particularly depressed about. Next, experiment by writing in the spaces provided the interpretations—positive, neutral, and negative—you might have of the same situation.

Positive thinking   *Neutral thinking*   *Negative thinking*

_____   _____   _____

_____   _____   _____

_____   _____   _____

"THIS IS THE WORST"

Now, examine the thoughts you wrote under the *Negative thinking* column. You might find them filled with exaggerations, with negative words such as "awful," "horrible," "terrible," "the worst." Or you might find that you've made unrealistic demands on yourself by using terms such as "should" or "must." When we feel depressed, our negative thoughts usually devalue our worth, paint a bleak future, and color our world in shades of black and gray. We do this by

- making unrealistic demands on ourselves or others
- negatively exaggerating unpleasant or inconvenient circumstances
- excusing ourselves from making constructive changes in our behavior

To gain insight into ways we do these three things to ourselves, please complete the following sentences. Write down your insights in the blank space following each sentence.

- I've made unrealistic demands on myself when I think I should

_____

- An example of taking an unpleasant event and making it into a catastrophe was when I

_____

• The last time I gave up was when I excused my behavior by

_____

Changing our thinking

In order to ease our discomfort and depression, we need to think, feel, and behave in our best interests. As we begin the recovery process, our goals are to increase our capacity for joy and contentment while minimizing our pain. We will look at a systematic way of learning how to change negative thinking to thoughts that are more realistic and neutral. It is an opportunity to apply some of the principles you've already learned.

First, let's begin by identifying our thoughts, feelings, and behaviors. To help us along the way, we will use a simple format: *A* represents the *event* associated with our depressed mood; *B* represents the negative or irrational *thoughts* that trigger and reinforce our depressed *feelings* at *C*.

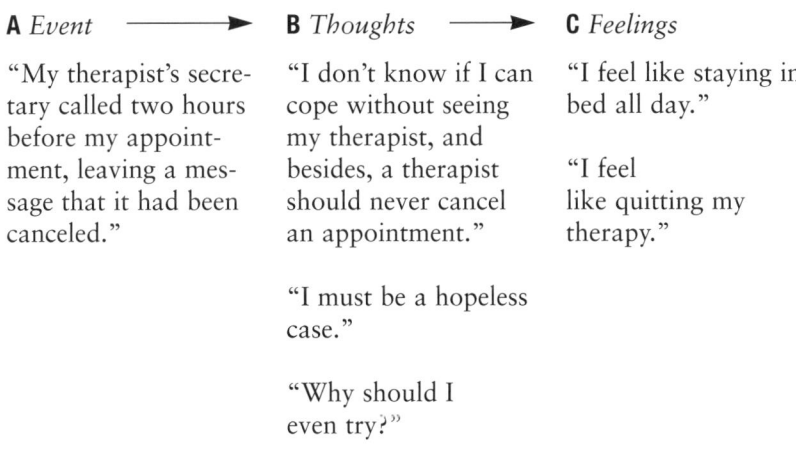

A *Event* ⟶ **B** *Thoughts* ⟶ **C** *Feelings*

"My therapist's secretary called two hours before my appointment, leaving a message that it had been canceled."

"I don't know if I can cope without seeing my therapist, and besides, a therapist should never cancel an appointment."

"I must be a hopeless case."

"Why should I even try?"

"I feel like staying in bed all day."

"I feel like quitting my therapy."

Now it's time to study an example of an event that set off a chain reaction of negative thoughts and feelings for you.

A: *The event*

Write in the following blank space, describing one event or situation. First, record just the facts. Avoid impressions or assumptions.

_____

_____

_____

B: *Thoughts (Inventory)*

Now you're ready to inventory your thoughts. Consider unrealistic demands and negative exaggerations. Often these include such words as *awful* and *terrible* in addition to *must's* and *should's*. Consider all internal thoughts that say *must, should,* or *it's terrible*. Write your inventory of unrealistic demands and negative thoughts in the space provided.

_____

_____

_____

C: *Feelings*

Next, describe your feelings that resulted from your negative thoughts.

_____

_____

_____

Urges-behavior

List any urges or behaviors that were linked to your feelings.

_____

_____

_____

Dispute and beyond!

The next step in the process is to *dispute* our negative beliefs. We'll do this by continuing with our simple format.

- *D* represents disputing our logic.
- *E* represents the goals that we establish for change.
- *F* represents the action plan to help make our goals a reality.

D entails a debate, where we actually question our logic. Usually, when we dispute our logic, we ask ourselves such questions as "Who said so?" "Where is my evidence?" "Can I prove it?" We replace our negative thoughts with more objective or neutral interpretations. Let's continue with our first example by questioning our logic.

- I've missed appointments before and have done fine. Who says a therapist should never cancel an appointment? That is my expectation. Maybe the therapist had no other choice but to cancel.
- What evidence do I have that I am a hopeless case? Who says there is a relationship between the canceled appointment and my ability to change?
- Giving up is an excuse that robs me of trying something new. Maybe this is an opportunity to fill that time slot with something new and interesting.

Now it's your turn. Applying the principles that you have learned and using the situation you worked out in *A*, *B*, and *C*, question your logic at *D*. Write in the blank space. Don't be afraid to debate your negative beliefs. Expect it to seem strange at first. When we try something new, it often feels a bit foreign.

D: *Questioning*

_____

_____

E and F—Goal and action plan

At *E* we have an opportunity to establish our goals. By questioning our *logic*, we've managed to reduce the intensity of our feelings of depression. That helps us to consider our situation more objectively. Now we need to answer the question, What would I like to have happen?

- Stop my self-defeating behavior while learning to cope with my feelings of depression

E: *Goal*

Now it's time to continue with *your* example. Establish your goal at *E*. What would you like to see happen? What is your preference for this situation? Develop a goal that helps you to become more content while reducing your distress. Describe it in the space provided.

_____

_____

_____

As we question our logic and set more realistic goals, the next step is to identify specific *actions* we can take to reach our goals. This process involves not only challenging our logic but also changing our behavior and taking action. At *F* we list the actions we can take to reach the goal we listed in section *E*.

- Call my therapist to reschedule. Inquire about the reason for the cancellation.
- Call a friend from my support group. Go out for coffee.
- Go for a walk, explore a new store opening in the neighborhood, exercise.
- Complete at least two more REBT assignments to change my self-depreciation and look for alternatives to giving up or running away.

F: *Actions I could take*
Now brainstorm all of the actions you could take to reach your goal. Write them in the space provided. Here you want to focus on behaving in your own best interests.

_____

_____

_____

_____

_____

_____

_____

At this point we have listed a few constructive activities to help us cope with our feelings of depression instead of returning to bed or hiding in our room. By the way, isolation is often a great time for relapsing into our old pattern of addiction. For some of us, feelings of depression, isolation, and drinking (or, for that matter, binge eating, other drug use, or compulsive sexual behavior) all seem to go hand-in-hand. REBT can help us to avoid these self-defeating behaviors.

Putting it into practice

Now that you have worked through an example, you have a foundation to build on. The REBT self-help method is relatively simple once you get the hang of it. But it only works if you apply the principles. Most people agree that you need to work through a number of examples before REBT becomes an easy process. More than likely, some of your negative beliefs are "old friends" that have been around for some time. Don't give up. Plan to apply some of these principles during the course of the day or write out an example tonight. Remember, once you have the skill, you can use it whenever it is needed. Try it. It works! Following is a worksheet to get you started.

REBT worksheet

A: *The event*

Writing in the following blank space, describe the situation. Record just the facts. Avoid impressions or assumptions.

_____

_____

_____

B: *Thoughts*

List an inventory of your thoughts. Consider unrealistic demands and negative exaggerations.

_____

_____

_____

C: *Feelings*
Describe your feelings that result from your negative thoughts.
Include any urges or behaviors that were linked to your feelings.

_____

_____

_____

D: *Questioning our shame-based logic*
Question your logic. Dispute your negative beliefs. Don't be
afraid to debate some of your negative beliefs. Ask questions such
as "Who said so?" and "Where is my evidence?"

_____

_____

_____

E: *Preferences or goals*
Establish new, realistic goals. What would you like to have happen? Develop a goal that helps you to increase your capacity for
contentment while reducing your distress. Describe your goal in
the space provided.

_____

_____

_____

F: *Actions I could take*
Brainstorm all the actions you could take to achieve your goals
listed in *E*. Focus on behaving in your own best interests. List
your goals.

_____

_____

_____